How Animals Move Around

By Zita and Aurora Hilvert-Bruce

Contents

Introduction	4
Moving on Land	6
Moving Through Water	12
Why Does a Water Strider Float?	16
Moving Through the Air	18
"The Albatross"	19
Just Like Animals!	23
Questions	24
Glossary	24
Index	25

Introduction

Animals move in many ways because they have different shapes.

Horses have long legs to gallop over land.

Fish have fins to swim through the water.

Birds have wings to fly through the air.

Many animals move
in more than one kind of way.

Some seals use their flippers
to move over land
and to swim through water.

Ducks can fly through the air
or walk on land.
They can also swim and dive.

Moving on Land

Many animals that live on land
have four legs.
They use all their legs
to lift their bodies off the ground.
This makes it easy for them
to walk and run.

Some animals have four legs, but stand on only two of them.

Sometimes bears walk on their back legs. They don't always need to use four legs.

Kangaroos have powerful back legs and feet for hopping.
They use their tails to help them balance as they hop.

Snakes have no legs at all.
They use muscles along their bodies
to push themselves forward.

This snake slides from side to side
over sandy ground.

Some animals climb trees.

Squirrels have claws
on their feet
for hanging on to branches.
They use their tails
for balancing as they climb.

DID YOU KNOW?

Monkeys have hands and feet
that grip the branches.
Some monkeys use their tails
to hang on.

Moles often dig tunnels through the ground when they are looking for food.

They dig with their strong front legs and big claws.

Moles have streamlined bodies, which make it easy for them to tunnel.

Moving Through Water

Animals that live in water
have streamlined bodies, too.
This helps them move smoothly
through the water.

Fish have fins for swimming.
The tail fin moves from side to side
to push away the water.
Other fins help them steer
and balance.

Seals have flippers for swimming.
Some seals use their front flippers
to row through the water.
Their flippers work like the oars of a boat.

DID YOU KNOW?

Penguins cannot fly.
They use their wings
to swim.

Some animals have webbed feet.

Ducks and frogs use their webbed feet to push themselves forward when they are swimming.

Insects have other ways
of moving through water.

The water strider skates over ponds.
It uses its middle pair of legs
to move forward,
and its back pair to steer.

DID YOU KNOW?

The backswimmer is an insect
that swims on its back.

Experiment

Why Does a Water Strider Float?

A water strider is shaped like a needle. Find out what happens when you put a needle on top of water.

You will need:
- a bowl
- a jug of water
- a small, dry needle

What to do:
1. Pour the water slowly into the bowl until it is nearly full.

2. Put the needle carefully on top of the water. Watch what happens.

What did you see?
Does the needle float or sink?

Try blowing on the needle to move it around.

Moving Through the Air

Most birds can fly.
They have strong muscles
that move their wings.
Birds push themselves through the air
by flapping their wings.

Birds are streamlined in shape.
Their light bones also help them to fly.

Some birds can glide through the air. The albatross is a bird that glides on sea winds.

The Albatross

*Albatross gliding
Above the waves of the sea.
Oh, so majestic!*

Rosemary Hurley

Bats have wings for flying.
Their wings are made of a very thin skin.
The skin joins a bat's fingers to its legs.

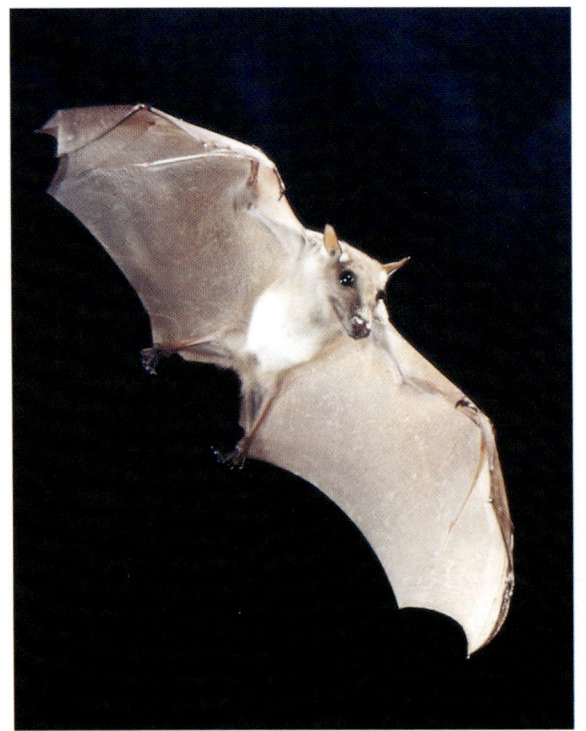 

When a fruit bat
hangs upside down to sleep,
it folds its wings around its body.

A flying squirrel also has a thin skin that joins its front leg to its back leg.

Flying squirrels cannot fly.
They glide between trees,
from a high branch to a low branch.

Many insects have two pairs of wings that they use for flying.

The front wings of a butterfly cover some of the back wings. The wings beat together when it flies.

DID YOU KNOW?

Dragonflies can fly backward.

Just Like Animals!

hang glider

submarine

plane

Do you know which animals move like these machines?

Questions

1. How do monkeys climb?
2. What do penguins use for swimming?
3. Which insect swims on its back?
4. Which insect can fly backward?

Glossary

balance	to be steady
fin	a part of a fish that is used for swimming
muscle	a part of the body that helps an animal move
streamlined	smoothly shaped, to make it easy to move
webbed feet	feet with a thin skin that joins the toes